JOURNALING PROMPTS

After the Loss of an Infant

THIS JOURNAL IS IN MEMORY OF:

AGED:

DUE DATE:

THIS JOURNAL

Dear Reader,

First, I am so sorry for your loss. It must be so hard.

Second, this book is designed for you. This journal is designed to be a framework for you to process some of what you are feeling after experiencing the loss of a baby.

It is not meant to be a replacement for the support you may need from friends or family. Nor does it offer the same benefits that professional counseling offers. This book is not meant to give you the peace you may find from a higher power. But this book may compliment any or all of those things, or help when you just can't get support in those other areas, for whatever reason.

I wrote this book so that you know you are not alone. Your grief is unique, as are your specific experiences. Your story is worth exploring. The prompts are designed for you to reflect and crystalize some of what you are feeling. I hope you find safety in your journaling. I hope that through some of the prompts, that you begin to heal.

Grief is not something that can be neatly wrapped in a bow. By the end of this journal, you will still have your grief. But it is my hope that as you work through the following pages, your grief feels a little lighter.

With Love,
The Author

YOUR BABY

Take some time to write about your baby.

The first few prompts will help you reflect on your baby's life and the memories you will carry of them.

DATE:

How did it feel when you found out you were pregnant? Who did you tell first?

_____

_____

_____

_____

_____

_____

_____

_____

_____

_____

_____

_____

_____

_____

_____

_____

_____

_____

_____

_____

DATE:

How did you first find out you were pregnant?

_____

_____

_____

_____

_____

_____

_____

_____

_____

_____

_____

_____

_____

_____

_____

_____

_____

_____

_____

_____

DATE:

What were some things that you sensed about your baby when they were in utero?

DATE:

What were some of your first hopes and dreams you had for your baby?

DATE:

What did you plan your family to look like? Were there any holidays, traditions, or trips you dreamed of?

DATE:

What was your baby's name? How was that name chosen?

_____

_____

_____

_____

_____

_____

_____

_____

_____

_____

_____

_____

_____

_____

_____

_____

_____

_____

DATE:

What will you remember most about being pregnant?

DATE:

When I close my eyes and picture my baby, I see...

_____

_____

_____

_____

_____

_____

_____

_____

_____

_____

_____

_____

_____

_____

_____

_____

_____

DETAILS

Write about as many details of your baby's birth and death as you feel comfortable with. If there is a prompt that feels too hard to answer, skip it.

This journal is a safe space for you. You will write if and when you are ready. Remember, there are no right or wrong answers. Blank spaces are allowed.

DATE:

Can you describe the story of your baby's birth and death? What happened that day?

DATE:

Who was with you?

DATE:

Besides the people with you at the time of your
baby's death, who did you tell first? Did you tell
them right away?

DATE:

What were your initial feelings when telling other people?

_____

_____

_____

_____

_____

_____

_____

_____

_____

_____

_____

_____

_____

_____

_____

_____

_____

_____

DATE:

What emotions have come up for you in the time that has followed?

DATE:

Were you able to hold your baby? If so, what will you remember most about that?

DATE:

My body feels...

_____

_____

_____

_____

_____

_____

_____

_____

_____

_____

_____

_____

_____

_____

_____

_____

_____

_____

DATE:

Do you still have more questions about your baby's death?

_____
_____
_____
_____
_____
_____
_____
_____
_____
_____
_____
_____
_____
_____
_____
_____
_____

RELATIONSHIPS

The next few prompts will help you to consider the support you have gotten from your partner, or what support has been lacking.

If you do not have a partner, you may choose to respond to the prompts as you feel. You may also choose to skip them.

DATE:

What people have been your main supports to you during this time?

DATE:

How has your partner given you support?

_____

_____

_____

_____

_____

_____

_____

_____

_____

_____

_____

_____

_____

_____

_____

_____

_____

_____

_____

DATE:

How has your partner been dealing with the death of your baby?

DATE:

How have you been able to support your partner?

_____

_____

_____

_____

_____

_____

_____

_____

_____

_____

_____

_____

_____

_____

_____

_____

DATE:

How has your partner been throughout this process?
Do they seem able to both grieve on their own and
grieve with you?

DATE:

How have they been grieving? How has that felt for you?

DATE:

Who else in your circle has been grieving for you and your family?

What has the grief of non-family members looked like? How does that feel to you?

DATE:

How does it feel to know other people are grieving for you?

_____
_____
_____
_____
_____
_____
_____
_____
_____
_____
_____
_____
_____
_____
_____
_____
_____
_____
_____
_____

DATE:

What is something that you wish your partner understood?

DATE:

What is something that you wish others around you understood?

DATE:

If you have social media, how have you handled those platforms lately?

DATE:

What have you and your partner talked about? What havent you talked about?

DATE:

What are your hopes and fears for you and your partner as you move forward?

DATE:

Do you have other children? How have they been during this time?

DATE:

Write a letter to your partner:

YOUR FEELINGS

You. Your grief. No one knows exactly how you feel, but the next few pages are designed for you to help sort out your thoughts and feelings for your own purposes.

If you are not ready, you can always skip a page and come back later when it feels better. Your experiences are valid and you are allowed to feel exactly as you do.

This is your story.

DATE:

When do you feel saddest?

How do you cope with numbness?

DATE:

Have you experienced anger? What does that look like?

DATE:

Have you experienced jealousy? How has that manifested?

DATE:

Do you experience a range of emotions all at once or
do you feel them separately from each other?

DATE:

What thoughts do you keep coming back to?

_____

_____

_____

_____

_____

_____

_____

_____

_____

_____

_____

_____

_____

_____

_____

_____

_____

DATE:

Is there anything that helps you focus your thoughts?

DATE:

What has felt the most raw?

_____
_____
_____
_____
_____
_____
_____
_____
_____
_____
_____
_____
_____
_____
_____
_____
_____
_____

DATE:

Thoughts I know are not true but I can't help from thinking are:

DATE:

The thing I hate to admit most is:

DATE:

The hardest part emotionally has been:

_____

_____

_____

_____

_____

_____

_____

_____

_____

_____

_____

_____

_____

_____

_____

_____

_____

_____

_____

DATE:

Where in your body do you feel the loss the most?

_____

_____

_____

_____

_____

_____

_____

_____

_____

_____

_____

_____

_____

_____

_____

_____

DATE:

What have you been doing to heal?

DATE:

Are you being patient with yourself in your healing process?

DATE:

Where have you found small moments of joy?

_____

_____

_____

_____

_____

_____

_____

_____

_____

_____

_____

_____

_____

_____

_____

_____

_____

_____

_____

_____

DATE:

How have you been reorienting yourself? Where do you go from here?

DATE:

Do you think you will ever feel the same? How will
you be changed by this?

_____

_____

_____

_____

_____

_____

_____

_____

_____

_____

_____

_____

_____

_____

_____

_____

DATE:

Write a letter to your baby.

AFTERWARD

In the months and years that followed your loss, you will continue to keep going.

This section will help you reflect on the events after your loss and your emotions surrounding them.

DATE:

My most trusted people throughout this have been:

DATE:

Did you recieve any hopeful comments from friends
or family after you told them about your baby?

DATE:

Did you recieve any hurtful comments from friends
or family after you told them about your baby?

DATE:

What has given you hope during this season of life?

_____
_____
_____
_____
_____
_____
_____
_____
_____
_____
_____
_____
_____
_____
_____
_____
_____
_____

DATE:

What gives you comfort?

DATE:

How have you felt healing? What activities feel soul soothing?

DATE:

What kindness have you been shown during this
time? Who has shown you love?

DATE:

What are some comforting words that you have found meaning in?

DATE:

What are some songs or artists that you have been
listening to a lot lately? Do any specific lines stand
out to you?

DATE:

What are you grateful for?

DATE:

What other resorces have felt helpful, even if only a little?

_____

_____

_____

_____

_____

_____

_____

_____

_____

_____

_____

_____

_____

_____

_____

_____

DATE:

Write a letter to yourself.

NOTES:

If you need more space to finish any prompts or just need to answer your own questions, continue writing here.

Made in the USA
Monee, IL
02 November 2024

69192614R00059